COWGIRL SPIRIT

Strong Women,
Solid Friendships
and Stories
from the Frontier

COWGIRL SPIRIT

Strong Women, Solid Friendships and Stories from the Frontier

◆Mimi Kirk◆

SOURCEBOOKS, INC.®
NAPERVILLE, ILLINOIS

Published by Sourcebooks, Inc.
P.O. Box 4410, Naperville, Illinois 60567-4410
(630) 961-3900
FAX: (630) 961-2168

Library of Congress Cataloging-in-Publication Data
Kirk, Mimi.
Cowgirl spirit: strong women, solid friendships and stories from the frontier/ by Mimi Kirk.
    p. cm.
    ISBN 1-57071-770-2 (alk. paper)
    1. Cowgirls—West(U.S.)—History—Miscellanea. 2. Cowgirls—West(U.S.)—Social life and customs—
    Miscellanea. 3. Cowgirls—West(U.S.)—Biography—Miscellanea. 4. Frontier and pioneer life—
    West(U.S)—Miscellanea. 5. Ranch life—West(U.S.)—Miscellanea. 6. West(U.S.)—Social life and customs—
    Miscellanea. I. Title.

F596 .K585 2001
978—dc21   00-024733

Printed and bound in the United States of America
VHG 10 9 8 7 6 5 4 3 2 1

Dedication

This book is dedicated to my mother, Dorothy; my children, Lisa, Jonas, Mia, and Dan; my daughters-in-law, Toni and Gigi; my son-in-law Hunter; my grandchildren, Mackenzie, Hannah, Karly, Rocco, and Luke; and my sisters, Arlene and Sydell. It is because of you I've learned unconditional love.

Acknowledgments

Heartfelt thanks to cowgirls Melody Swan and Melissa Haye–Cserhat for helping me in the creation of the *Cowgirls Ride the Trail of Truth* board game for women. Blessings on Mary Burns and all the investors who gave the game its wings.

This book could not have been written without the generosity of the women I interviewed and the women of the past who kept journals to record their lives. I thank each and every one of you for the time and energy you gave to make this book possible.

Without references and the work of others' research, a book like this could not be written. I want to express my appreciation to the Wyoming Division of Cultural Resources for their continued support in all my endeavors.

Working with my editor, Deb Werksman, was a revelation and a delight. With your good spirits, wisdom, and humor, you taught me how to put a book together. I thank Dominique Raccah, president of Sourcebooks, for taking me into her trust and publishing this book.

And thanks to Mia White for doing such a wonderful job with transcribing my taped interviews, considering all the tape machine problems I encountered. I know you worked late into the night, and I always know I can trust you to complete any project the perfect way.

Warmth and affection to my generous writer friends Pat Nardo, who read all my drafts and helped me stay within the lines. It would have been harrowing without you. And Ziggy

Steinberg, you gave me insights on how to write a story and kept me laughing along the way.

My family and girlfriends deserve enormous kudos. They were always by my side, listening to my personal stories and tired voice over and over, and always making me feel I could do no wrong. You are my true gal pals, Lisa Kirk, Mia White, Toni Kirk, Julie Kavner, Kathy Christianson, Maria Rosa Alvarez-Calderon, and Tricia Joyce.

And to the kindest gentleman I know, Bob Conley, whose knowledge I am constantly marveled by. You are my mentor and my source of strength. You give me encouragement, and constant support, and your generosity of my laptop made this book possible to write. I hold you in high esteem and I am deeply grateful. You are the angel on my shoulder.

Table of Contents

Introduction

Years ago, I was strolling in a small town in the South of France with an author friend, Jerzy Kosinski, who wrote, among other works of literature, *The Painted Bird* and *Being There*. We saw a wedding party coming out of a church. It was quite a beautiful old church, built in the 1800s, and I felt that we were privy to a very special moment in someone else's life. Jerzy took some photos, and we rushed off to meet several people for lunch. During the meal, in an outdoor cafe, Jerzy started to tell a story about a woman in a white dress standing in a graveyard with flowers in her hand. The story was captivating and we were all spellbound and on the edge of our chairs when I suddenly realized that he was talking about the same wedding party we had seen coming out of the church an hour before. I was so amazed that we saw the same occurrence and he knew how to pluck out the special and colorful moments and make them mesmerizing. It was true, he saw the irony in the fact that the graveyard was positioned next to the path the bride and groom were walking on. He saw faces and created stories for them, he truly knew how to make life interesting. In that moment, Jerzy taught me to see beyond the obvious and into the essence of life. Everyone's life is interesting.

Women of the frontier recorded and reflected on their lives by writing in their diaries and journals. I'm sure at the time it was the only way to process their thoughts and feelings. Many women of that era were illiterate—we will never know the full stories of those women's lives. In reading the accounts that exist, however, we can see frontier women's lives as historical and interesting, and in the telling of our own lives, we discover who we are.

Life was hard on the frontier, and women were hungry for each other's company, just as women today find strength and inspiration in our female friends. When women were able to get together back then, they talked, gossiped, and exchanged recipes, ideas, and feelings. Women on the trail lived with limited water supplies, unsanitary conditions, and little privacy, but they were very skilled in caring. They delivered children, set broken bones, and found healing herbs on the trail. No matter how barren their circumstances, these women found a way. They made do, and did whatever was needed. They still cared about their appearance, even in the wilderness, and used hot pokers and rags to curl their hair. The advent of mail-order brought wonderful surprises of ribbons, sachets, hair tonics, and wrinkle-smoothers.

As women became more confident, they struck out for paying occupations, such as social service, teaching, and nursing, and a surprising number ran their own ranches or made a living breaking horses. Today, women face less resistance if we choose to work outside of the home. We are doctors, lawyers, athletes, businesswomen, scientists, journalists, teachers, and politicians. We work in every field that men do. We now are in positions of leadership, opportunity, and recognition. We work hard to improve ourselves personally and professionally. Women have made a major transformation and our lives will never be the same again. We pay tribute to the women of the past and go forward with our own expeditions and pioneering. They survived and we survive, and we will continue to make life better for ourselves and for the next generation of women.

Women have come a long way since the frontier, and this book is a thread that joins us together, a kinship in a way. *Cowgirl Spirit* contains stories about women of the past and women of today who live in high spirits.

There are countless possibilities for women's lives. The women in these stories define women of yesterday and today, our similarities, and the long, long way we have come in our struggles for independence, confidence, happiness, and love.

Cowgirl Spirit is meant to inspire women and girls of all ages. Journey beyond your wildest dreams and make a difference in the world. Don't be afraid to make mistakes, and even if you fail, other women will try because you did. Speak out for what you believe, saturate yourself with love, and experience your life as a fascinating adventure.

Chapter One
Independence

How could anyone look me in the eye and
say I'm not independent?
—Mildred Shaw, 1886

Then...

At the time of Dr. Bethenia Owens–Adair's death at eighty–six years old, she was recognized for her achievements in her career. It is remarkable that she became a doctor in a time when women were not eagerly accepted into the medical profession, and education was not readily available to them at all.

Dr. Bethenia Owens–Adair was born on February 7, 1840. When she turned three, her family left Mississippi and were among early settlers who emigrated west on the famous Oregon Trail.

There were no schools with regular sessions, and Bethenia was always anxious to learn more. When she was twelve, a teacher came to the community for three months. It was the only formal education Bethenia received until several years later.

Bethenia married at thirteen. Her husband, Legrand Hill, was fourteen. They bought a twelve–by–fourteen foot cabin without floors or a chimney. Bethenia cooked outside even when it rained. Their household consisted of a cooking pot, a teakettle, an oven, a twenty–gallon iron pot for heating water, a washtub scrubbing board, six milk pans, and a churn. Bethenia soon gave birth to a son they named George.

Cowgirl Spirit

Unlike her husband, who was lazy, Bethenia was a hard worker. Legrand was quick-tempered and abusive to Bethenia. After she could take it no more, she left Legrand and moved in with her parents.

Bethenia was hungry for more education so she could take care of herself and her son. When a school opened near the family home, Bethenia left George with her younger brothers and sisters so she could attend classes.

She milked the cows and did the housework each morning before going to school. On weekends, she washed and ironed. Bethenia earned her living by sewing and doing home nursing and washing.

She moved to Oysterville, Washington, where she had a friend, and began to teach school. Determined to support herself and George, she lined up sixteen children whose parents paid her a monthly tuition of three dollars.

Bethenia would work all day and study at night because a few of her pupils were more advanced than she was. She never had a full night's sleep, and eventually gave up teaching to further her studies.

Setting up housekeeping in a small space, Bethenia sewed, crocheted, took in washing, sold firewood, which she picked up on the beach, and earned a total of five dollars a week. She continued studying along with her daily chores. Bethenia eventually set up a millinery and dressmaking business. Although she found plenty of work, Bethenia was not satisfied, as she preferred to take care of the sick. She came to the decision to become a doctor, although she knew it was not an easy road. Turning her successful business over to her sister and putting her fourteen-year-old son in college, she went to Philadelphia to attend medical school.

This horrified friends and relatives, as there were no female doctors. They thought it a disgrace and tried to persuade her to abandon the idea. Bethenia left to study anyway and earned her degree, but could only practice medicine to a certain extent because of her limited training.

Shortly after Bethenia arrived back home, the local physicians were conducting an autopsy on an old man who had died. To embarrass Bethenia, they invited her to take part, thinking she would never show up. Of course she did. Dr. Hoover, one of the physicians, greeted her with a question as she entered the room. "Do you know the autopsy is on the genital organs?"

"No, but one part of the human body should be as sacred to the physician as another," she said.

Another doctor said, "I object to a woman being present at a male autopsy, and if she is allowed to remain, I will leave."

Bethenia replied, "I came here by written invitation and will leave it to a vote whether I go or stay, but first I would like to ask Dr. Palmer what the difference is between the attendance of a woman at a male autopsy and the attendance of a man at a female autopsy?"

One of the doctors left and the remaining doctors handed her the instruments to do the dissection.

When Bethenia had finished, the attending audience cheered her. News of her success traveled through town as she walked home. Men, women, and children came out to take a look at the woman who dared to carry on such a strange action. The town could have tarred and feathered her, feelings ran so high.

Bethenia, now thirty-eight years old, applied to attend Jefferson College in Philadelphia, a school that had never accepted a woman. Her application was refused. After a long search, she was accepted at the University of Michigan. After two years at the university, she received a bona fide medical degree.

Bethenia married Colonel John Adair in 1884. A short time later, she had a baby girl who only lived for three days. Bethenia was grief stricken. For health reasons, John wanted Bethenia to move to a farm. For eleven years she remained there treating the sick in out-of-the-way places. She never refused anyone her services night or day, whether they had money or not.

When Bethenia finally retired, she wrote letters to newspapers and spoke to thousands of women at temperance meetings. Bethenia lobbied successfully for a bill that changed the age of sexual consent for prostitution from the age of fourteen to sixteen. She was remembered not only for her accomplishments in the medical profession but for her dedication to social causes.

If I don't look out for my own well-being, no one else will. —R.B. Farmer, 1887

Now...

It all started with a radio contest that was held for long-haired girls by Clairol Long and Silky. Joan Severance of Houston, Texas, entered because she wanted to win a stereo of her own. She was tired of listening to her parents' music selections. Joan lost first place to Rene Russo, but won the third place prize of a modeling scholarship. She didn't see the value in this, but her mother forced her to take the gift, thinking it would help her daughter balance her reclusive nature. But Joan didn't see herself as reclusive, just independent. She enjoyed her solitude, and never felt lonely. As a girl, she was more concerned about her school grades than social activities.

Joan attended modeling school while she was a senior in high school. Her classic beauty was recognized early when her modeling teacher entered her in the Miss Houston Contest, where she lost first place, but won Miss Photogenic and captured the attention of John Casablanca of the Elite Modeling Agency. He saw her photo and sent her a ticket to Paris to become a model.

At first, Joan thought the offer was a joke, but her concerns were unfounded. John Casablanca was legitimate. She decided to accept his modeling offer to earn money for college.

Alone, Joan traveled to Paris that summer and never stopped working. Needless to say, she found herself in a world far different from the one she knew in Texas. Joan quickly went from the only job she ever had, which was babysitting, to being a top model. Only in retrospect did she grasp how exciting it was. Her independent spirit stood her in good stead living so far from home and immersed in so many new experiences.

Eventually, Joan left Paris to pursue her modeling career in New York. However, when she arrived there, modeling trends had changed. Instead of the popular European look that Joan represented, American blondes were "in." It took two years for Joan's look to be back in fashion again, and she finally started getting calls to work in television commercials. She had great success doing national spots, and at the same time her experience in front of the camera gave her the ability to teach commercial acting classes.

As if her modeling and commercial career didn't keep her busy enough, Joan was always on the path of independence and self-sufficiency. She opened a catering company called Good Food Catering, and eventually opened a restaurant/ bed and breakfast in upstate New York. It was a weekend spot, which she called Tequila. Among other responsibilities, Joan was the chef.

Joan would model all week, then leave the city on Thursday afternoon to go up to the restaurant and prepare the food. She would manage the inn throughout the weekend and go back to the city on Monday to pick up her modeling assignments.

Because Joan grew up with her parents telling her that the word "can't" doesn't exist, it's what she's always believed. "It doesn't mean that everything is always going to work," says Joan, "but it has all the possibilities of working. I just have to figure out how to do it." That "can do" attitude is a big part of an independent spirit, Joan is convinced. "You're not looking around for someone else to live your life for you," she says, "you're making the most out of every moment yourself."

Chapter Two

Friendship

I've never met a women that I didn't have
something in common with.

—Iris Martin, 1885

Then...

It was lonely for many women on the frontier as homesteads were sometimes miles apart from the closest neighbor. It was especially lonely in winter when the twenty-degree-below-zero weather kept people inside for months at a time. It was different for women traveling in wagon trains, since the slow-moving wagons allowed a unique camaraderie among them.

Quilting bees were what women most looked forward to. While sewing patches for a quilt, women could socialize. Although a wife's duties on the ranch didn't allow her much time for recreation, quilts were necessary for family warmth. It justified the all-day time that the women spent together. Women came from miles in all directions to help assemble the pieces of the quilt. It was a time of laughter and a time when oneliness disappeared.

Women spoke about dress patterns, recipes, families, and, of course, just plain gossip. They shared secrets of buttermilk and cornstarch to soften their skin. They talked about wrinkle-smoothers and tonics made from elderflower water and tannic acid. They spoke of the fashions of the big city and they talked about the things they could not discuss with their men. Deep friendships were made, and the women helped each other when families were ill, when extra hands were needed for farming, when babies were delivered, and when barns were raised.

Anna Curry and Francis Wilson found they had much in common. They were both schoolteachers with families of their own and they were both barely older than their pupils. Narcissa Whitman and Eliza Spalding were missionary wives, separated by 120 miles. Because the mail sometimes took months or even years to arrive, the women decided to keep in touch psychically. Each morning at 9 A.M., they isolated themselves to meditate on their duties and to pray for the welfare and safety of their families. They would think of each other, and in this way they kept their friendship and connection.

It appeared that the friendlier women became with each other, the more they discovered their own talents and strengths. Harriet Strong said to a group of Suffragettes, "It takes brains, not brawn, to make farms pay. We need more women farmers!" After the first suffrage laws were passed in 1869, 10 percent of all homesteaders were women. Whatever had to be done, women found out they could do it.

Women also found out how much they needed each other. With the men gone for months at a time, isolation from other women was sometimes unbearable. Most of the literate pioneer women kept journals and diaries. These journals served as a place to express their emotions and loneliness, but nothing replaced the company of close female friends.

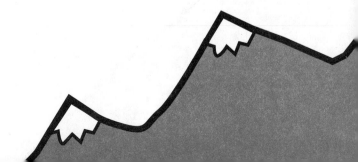

Now...

Jane Barthelemy grew up in a tight-knit family where cultural aspects of life were important. There were always music, art, and science projects going on at home, even though the family had very limited finances. Jane's lived in a quanset hut—metal buildings used by the military for housing and storage. Her family never owned anything that was new. Her mother sewed the family clothes and shopped at Salvation Army and Goodwill stores. Her father would stalk the streets looking for discarded furniture for their house. But, somehow, that didn't keep her mother from taking Jane and her sisters to every concert, ballet, and opera that was in town. Once, her mother even had the telephone removed just to get her deposit money back so she could take her daughters to a concert. Close friendship and camaraderie within the family was a vital part of Jane's growing up.

When Jane was in junior high school, her family moved from Minneapolis to Texas. It was a turbulent and emotional time for Jane, who had trouble making friends with the relatively privileged girls she was encountering. She missed her friends desperately. She was happy when the family moved once again to Boston.

Hold your tongue when it comes to talking badly about a friend. —Mary Lloyd, 1880

Jane played the violin for many years and found her niche with the best musicians at school. On Saturdays, she and her friends from Lexington, Massachusetts, would go to play in the All City Orchestra and the National Orchestra. Jane found that her friends pushed her to advance in her music, supported her through ups and downs, and were the people she could have the most fun with. Jane loved being surrounded by people who shared her love of music.

At Indiana University, Jane studied a general curriculum of music and languages, excelling in both, although she was devastated when the voice department turned down her audition. She learned Spanish, Russian, German, and an African dialect, graduating with degrees in music and Russian.

Companionship was always important to Jane. She married at nineteen and was very idealistic. When her marriage became disappointing, Jane started searching in other places for happiness. She met a spiritual teacher from New York, left her marriage, and moved into a Hindu religious community. Not since her days with her musician friends in high school did she feel so surrounded by like-minded and similarly purposeful friends.

The ashram started a successful restaurant called Taos and published a cookbook titled *The Tao of Cooking*. Jane worked in the restaurant for two years, then went to business school so she could help the business grow. She received her MBA and was the chief financial officer for ten years.

After that period, Jane was developing food allergies and began to feel discontented. Sensing it was time for a change, she left the ashram and hired a private voice teacher. Jane discovered in herself an enormous soprano voice and went off to New York. Shortly after that, she decided to go to Italy where she won a singing contest and actually began getting singing jobs. Jane sang soprano professionally for four years, during which time she toured the world, including Australia and South Africa, and sang in many great operas, including her favorite, *La Traviata*.

Although she loved her work, Jane was feeling the loneliness of a life not filled with friends, family, and community. It seemed to her that no matter how much she loved what she was doing and how much fun she was having, without her friends, there was something missing.

Jane moved back to the United States, and now lives near her ashram, where she can draw on the love, support, and like-mindedness of her friends. Jane stopped singing and opened a studio importing Venetian glass beads. She learned everything she needed to know about jewelry design, and now makes her living creating beautiful Venetian glass jewelry. She loves being her own boss and especially enjoys talking to her customers about her experiences as an opera singer in Italy. She made a CD of her opera arias that she plays at trade shows.

Jane says, "It doesn't matter what stage of life I'm in, my friends give me support and energy when life gets confusing."

Chapter Three

Confidence

I feel rooted to the earth like an old oak
tree and no one can move me.
—Nancy Park, 1897

When I am dedicated to something, I do it right.

Then...

Marietta Stow was the first woman ever nominated for Vice President of the United States. In fact, she was nominated twice, once in 1884 and the second time 1888. Marietta was persistent about making a difference. She ran for San Francisco school director in 1880 and for governor in 1882. When frontier women ran for office to publicize their cause, they did not expect to win because equal voting rights had not been adopted. Marietta received only fifteen votes when she ran for governor. She and her presidential running mate, Belva Lockwood, an attorney from Washington, D.C., received only four thousand votes cast for them in seven states. Although Marietta was never elected, even after four tries for the San Francisco school directorship, she wouldn't give up.

As a big supporter of dress reform, she always campaigned in attire of her own design—a skirt twelve inches from the floor. Underneath she wore stockings, trousers, or leggings. Marietta thought, along with other feminist women of that period, that long dresses were a sign of degradation. It is difficult for women who want to enjoy the beauty of the outdoors to do so in this unsuitable attire, she explained. It also limited them if they wanted to pursue the outdoor sports men enjoyed.

Marietta, never at a loss for words, continued to bring attention to the issues she thought important. She endorsed widow's rights, racial equality, physical culture, family communes, and the protection of suffrage.

Forthright and confident, she continued speaking out to both women and men, fearless of what they might have thought or said about her. Once, during a pause in a gentleman's speech, Marietta stood up and spoke out about women's suffrage. She held the floor long enough to get her point across to the assembly. When the speaker began to talk loudly to overcome Marietta, she sat down, content in knowing that she had accomplished her mission.

Marietta Stow lived just long enough to see the first efforts towards women's suffrage get underway.

Now...

Mona Brookes has gained international recognition as the creator of a revolutionary drawing method that has both children and corporations recognizing the value of visual skills for learning. Mona Brookes grew up in a poor family living in a three-story Victorian house with six other families. Her family of six lived in one room and shared a bathroom with three other families.

Mona was always a confident child, and it would be no surprise to anyone who knew her, even at the age of four, that she would grow up to do something special. Mona's mother, an avid reader, would borrow seven books from the library and read one each day of the week. Mona sat on her mother's lap as she read out loud and tracked the lines, not necessarily knowing what they meant.

By the time Mona was seven years old, she was considered a child prodigy. Not only could she read volumes of books, but she also could draw anything. By the age of ten, she was borrowing the same number of books as her mother and was reading them just as quickly. Any girl who was reading Gandhi at twelve had a different way of looking at the world.

One evening, looking up at the sky, Mona said to her

girlfriends, "Gee, to look at all the different planets and to know there is life out there is amazing." Well, that was it. Her friends told their parents that she said there were beings on other planets, and the parents saw that their children never spoke to Mona again.

Mona left home at seventeen and never saw any of her high school classmates again. Throughout her school years, Mona's teachers thought she could be a success story and they helped her obtain a scholarship to a top art school. She would find herself in classes where teachers were drawing over her pictures and telling her to do it a different way. One teacher contradicted the other, and all contradicted what she felt in her heart was the right way for her. Mona left art school to study psychology, graduated from college, and became a probation officer working with delinquent girls.

She was also a job counselor and a play therapist. She was happier now than she had ever been, as she felt that she was making a difference in the world. She sold her art to people who saw her work and wanted to buy it. After seventeen years of social work, Mona decided she was ready to resume her life as an artist. She withdrew her retirement funds, put her portfolio together, and began to teach children how to draw. She developed a now-famous drawing methodology that has changed the whole educational view on how to teach children to draw. Her methodology is used today in schools all over the world. The system is called the Monart Method.

After seeing Mona on the *Today Show*, a publisher encouraged her to write a book.

Confidence

Mona's books have had a profound effect on the lives of many people world-wide. She has thirty drawing schools around the country. Mona teaches workshops all over the United States. Hundreds of thousands of teachers use the Monart Method in their classrooms in curricula for math, science, history, social studies, and geography. Students taught with this method are scoring 20 percent higher on standardized tests. Children with attention-deficit disorders using the Monart Method can sit, absorbed in their lessons, for over an hour. There is no critique of their drawing. With Mona's method, there is no right or wrong way to do anything. "If you draw what you are learning, you learn it eight times faster and retain it eight times longer," Mona says. She felt that the critical teaching methods she had encountered were bad for people's confidence. She always relied on her own sense of self-confidence in building a wonderful life for herself. She always has been committed to helping others. Mona says that fostering confidence in a child is a great gift.

Chapter Four

Happiness

I want to seize any pleasure that comes my way because it might not come by again.
—Amelia Banks, 1901

Then...

Whereas most pioneer women lived in danger and hardship, Harriet Fenn found happiness, love, and protection in her marriage to Fisk Sanders of New York, a prosperous lawyer deeply devoted to his family.

Harriet was born in April, 1834. She was a week older than her husband. In 1863, because of ill health, Sanders took his family west on a wagon train of about seventeen people. They were moving west not for land or prosperity, but because that was where energetic and ambitious people went at that time.

Harriet and the other women loved being on the road and not having to keep house daily. They had time to take naps and relax while the wagons moved westward. Unlike most of the wagon trains before them, they had a wonderful time. They were not early travelers, so they had guide books telling them where food and water could be obtained and where there might be danger.

Harriet always looked on the bright side of life and made the trip enjoyable for everyone along. On June 20, 1863, she wrote, "I certainly have enjoyed the journey so far much better than I had expected. This afternoon I rode the pony and carried Jimmie for an hour and then walked three miles. The children are better on the trail than they were at home."

Harriet kept herself amused by admiring the lightning during rainstorms, collecting and pressing wildflowers, and counting telegraph poles. She would wash her dresses and sometimes pin them to the top of the wagon to dry as the wagon moved. She starched her sunbonnets and dried and shaped them over pillows.

Of course, there were rattlesnakes, extreme heat and cold, and Indians to be dealt with. There were the dangers of crossing rivers, oxen getting caught in quicksand, wagons overturning, and sickness. But, through any mishap, Harriet kept her lightness and sense of humor, which reflected on everyone in the wagon train.

One evening during a heavy rainstorm, Harriet and her sons went to their Aunt Mary's tent because it didn't leak quite as much as their wagon did. "There was no use crying," she wrote, "so we all went to singing, and such a time as we had. Mr. Booth [one of the drivers] said that after that demonstration we need not be afraid of Indians. He knew they would run if they heard us."

Several days later, Indians approached and asked for food. After they were given some, they brought back more Indians and demanded more food. The camp refused them and, led by Harriet, the group sat down and sang songs until the Indians left. This chain of events all occurred before Harriet's thirty-third birthday. Harriet and her family ultimately settled in Montana.

Happiness

Now...

Lucia Capacchione was always happy cutting things up and putting the pieces together. She came by this naturally, as her father was a film editor at MGM and her mother was a costume designer and dressmaker. Lucia spent many days on movie sets meeting movie stars. She loved that world, and would gather her neighborhood friends and put on plays in her garage.

She went to a Catholic girls school, where she studied with Sister Mary Corita, well-known for her work of modern art with a spiritual touch. During that time, Lucia was captivated with Charles Eames, the furniture designer, and was determined to work for him. She got herself a job with Eames working on exhibits, film showroom props, and film research. It was Sister Corita who encouraged her to teach and recommended her for a job in an inner city school with poor and immigrant children. Lucia felt unqualified, but plunged in knowing it would be a good experience.

She brought her art materials into the classroom and taught fractions by having the students cut things and glue them down on pieces of paper. In addition to learning their math, the children won art contests across the city.

Lucia stayed home for a period of time with her children, did some freelance design-ing, and enrolled in the Maria Montessori Teacher Training Program. Out of the blue, the Archdiocese offered her a job. Again, she felt unqualified to supervise a three hundred-child program with fifty teachers, but at twenty-nine, Lucia jumped in. She surprised herself that she could be an administrator, design a curriculum, and write her own teacher's manual. Her program was evaluated the second-best program in Los Angeles County. She was doing wonderful work and had established herself in the field of early childhood education when, suddenly, everything fell apart. Her marriage, along with that of her parents, ended. She became ill with mononucleosis, and began writing and drawing her feelings and dreams, seeking a way to rebuild the happiness that seemed, at the time, so elusive. She later discovered that what she was doing was called "art therapy," and that it really worked. After she recovered, Lucia earned a master's degree in art therapy, started her own practice, and taught people how to draw from the unconscious to write about their feelings and find happiness in their lives. She wrote her first book, *The Creative Journal: The Art of Finding Yourself.*

She is now the author of over a dozen books. Her latest, *Visioning: 10 Steps to Designing the Life of Your Dreams*, shows how to turn your dreams into physical reality. Lucia hosts personal-growth seminars and is an art therapist, author, workshop leader, and corporate consultant. Through collage-making and journaling she teaches

Happiness

people to turn their wishes into physical reality. Lucia is living in the dream house she created. She says, "If you can dream it, you can do it." Lucia believes that everyone can have a happy life if they have the tools to create one.

Chapter Five

Love

Wanted: Cowboy—
nice-looking, affectionate, and good natured.
—Mary Jane, 1875

Then...

Maria Virginia Slade, nicknamed Molly, would do anything for her man. She was married to Joseph Slade, a well-known killer, but she loved him dearly and was a loyal and faithful wife until his death.

Joseph was ruthless, but Molly overlooked his faults. Once, she saved his life when angry outlaws captured and isolated Joseph in a log cabin and planned to kill him. Joseph begged them to let his wife visit one last time. They agreed and Molly rushed into the cabin crying. Shortly after, Joe opened the door with a gun in each hand. Behind him was Molly with another gun. She had smuggled the pistols in under her flowing skirt and the couple was able to get away unharmed.

It was obvious to everyone that Molly had a big heart. When a widow was left with two children and had no one to turn to, Molly gave her half of her own dresses and remolded some of the clothes for the children.

Joe Slade continued his rampages. One night, a friend appeared at Molly's door to tell her that her husband was going to be hanged. Molly Slade was a terrific rider and had a famous horse named Billy Bay. She took off on Billy to make the rescue effort with her long black hair flying in the breeze. She traveled at breakneck speed, yelling like a wild woman as she rode the path to where the hanging was to take place. Molly arrived minutes too late to save her beloved husband. Joe had been hanged.

Completely broken-hearted, Molly ordered a zinc-lined coffin and filled it with alcohol as a preservative. Molly waited until spring, when the snow melted in the mountains, to bury Joe in a special cemetery in Salt Lake City, away from his enemies in Virginia City.

No one ever knew what happened to Molly Slade after that. Rumor had it that her ghost rides Billy Bay on the path from her home to the hanging spot over and over again with her wild black hair flying in the breeze.

Love

Now...

Alice Matskin had been divorced for seven years. She had two children and was blessed with good friends. She was content and felt her life was sweet, but she had a vision that someday she would travel around the world in the company of a loving man.

Then Alice met Richard at a party, and again on three different occasions after that. Alice invited Richard to go dancing with her. They danced like Fred Astaire and Ginger Rogers, and have been living together from that day forward.

Richard was studying and practicing Eastern philosophy and Alice traveled with him to India where the two were married by a Brahmin priest in a small village. They had a very unusual wedding and honeymooned in India.

They returned home to Alice's teenagers, and Richard melded right into the family. A few years later, they embarked on a thirteen-month trip around the world. Here Alice was, in her forties, in a deep and loving relationship, traveling to exotic places. It was her dream come true.

When they arrived home, the couple decided to move to the country. Alice took up painting and Richard, an artist in his own right, started sculpting. They were so close, even with their work, that each one could pick up where the other left off. Richard could jump right into Alice's painting and she could jump right into his sculpting.

Alice did about twenty-five paintings of people in her community, including one of Beatrice Wood, a famous potter who was one hundred years old at the time. A friend of Alice's suggested she contact the Smithsonian National Portrait Gallery to see if they would be interested in the portrait of Beatrice. The Smithsonian was interested, and sent an air-conditioned truck to transport the painting to Washington. Alice and Richard went to Washington for the installation. The curator told Alice if she ever painted anyone else famous to let them know.

Alice became involved with a project called "Woman of Age." She was painting women over seventy years old and asking them, "What makes life worthwhile?" Alice interviewed and painted Betty Friedan. She called the Smithsonian, the truck returned, and Alice now has two paintings hanging in the Smithsonian.

Alice began getting commissions. She painted a portrait of the actor Larry Hagman, and he liked her work. His wife invited Alice to paint a picture of Hillary Clinton as a gift from the Congressional Club to be presented to the First Lady at their yearly lecture. After considering the invitation, Alice suggested that a painting of Hillary's daughter, Chelsea, would make a better gift. The club accected her idea. Alice completed the painting, working from photos of Chelsea Clinton. She and Richard were brought to

33

I think love is the answer to a lot of things, like feeling lonely.

Washington to attend the luncheon, and the painting was hung in the White House.

Alice and Richard spend much of their time taking care of Richard's parents. They have lots of older people in their life, including Alice's mother. They feel there is much to learn about one's self from older folks.

Alice and Richard have been together for seventeen years, and it has been seventeen years of complete sweetness and love. They feel their relationship is as sweet and beautiful today as it was the minute they looked into each other's eyes and knew they were in love.

Chapter Six

Strength

I can carry everything I own in my buggy,
and I just might leave this place.
—Carrie Black, 1901

Then...

Carolyn Charles was born in the 1850s. She was not well educated, but was considered very bright by her family and friends. She was also considered a rabble-rouser and somewhat of a rebel. Ever since she was five, she had a passion for horses. Growing up, she spent all her time outside, hardly coming in for supper.

Her brothers had nothing on her when it came to roping or riding. Everyone knew Carolyn was a competitive girl. She was determined to win and to be the best at everything she did.

Carolyn earned money by breaking horses for ranchers. At seventeen, she wanted to own her own land and horses. Her father helped her purchase a small ranch not far from the family's land. Carolyn always knew where to gather wild horses to enlarge her stable.

One day, a tall good-looking cowboy stopped by Carolyn's ranch looking for horses. They spoke for hours as they had so much in common with their love for horses. Several months later, he asked to marry her. Carolyn agreed to marry Oklahoma cowboy Robert Conroy on one condition, that she would hold on to her part of the ranch

🌵 Cowgirl Spirit

and horses by keeping it in her name in case the marriage didn't work out. Robert agreed, sold his ranch in Oklahoma, moved his horses and belongings to Carolyn's ranch, and purchased the bordering land.

It seemed that Robert was more of a homemaker than Carolyn. She only wanted to be in the barn and in the pastures with the horses. Robert could handle any task at hand, in or out of the farmhouse. He did most of the cooking and most of the chores. He also loved to gather wild horses and break them, and was skilled at everything he did.

It was unusual to see a man in this time who did not mind doing women's work. Carolyn felt she really got the better of the deal with this union. She and Robert worked side-by-side building their horse trade business. Once this twosome set their mind on something, it was done. Robert kept the books and knew how to manage the money, and Carolyn's positive spirit kept them always looking to the bright side of life.

They shared the same love of life and had two children, who they nourished and adored. They were friendly folks and loved to help at barn raisings and attend social gatherings. At get-togethers, Robert would outshine the neighborhood women by bringing the best dish.

They had a reputation for good horsemanship and were always in competition with each other to see who could stay on the bucking horses the longest. They claimed it was for fun, but it was always a great source of pleasure to be the winner.

37

Strength

Since the cattle business was conducted on horseback, the horse business was growing stronger. The Conroy's horses were fed, trained, and sold at the right price, and their buyers were always satisfied with the quality and training the horses possessed.

Carolyn always held her ground when she believed in something and was one of the few women who refused to ride sidesaddle. She always rode astride and wore pants or a split skirt. Carolyn and Robert stayed on the ranch after their semi-retirement from the horse business and continued to ride long after most older folks had stopped. They died one week apart from each other at the ages of seventy-five and seventy-nine, respectively, rarely having left their land.

Cowgirl Spirit

Now...

Linda Parks is a pilot for American Airlines. Passengers frequently ask her for coffee, and it doesn't bother Linda because she gets equal pay for equal work. She also feels piloting is a much safer profession than her last one—training wild animals.

Linda had no ambitions growing up in a small town—the same one both her parents were raised in. She was expected to find a man, get married, and live a quiet life.

When the family moved to Florida, Linda discovered she was a better swimmer than any of the other kids. In fact, she won backyard races, beating both women and men. For Linda, it was all a lark, even taking second place in three events at the public pool didn't feel like any big deal to her. Her athleticism came naturally and without any training. She took up skiing, and again won any race she entered.

By the time she got to college, she began to notice that boys had pressure on them to "make something of themselves" since they were expected to be the breadwinners. She was relieved she didn't have to worry about that. Since there were no expectations put on her, anything she did well received much praise. She even had the fun of activities such as throwing a football or skiing with everyone marveling at her, "That's great for a girl."

Her grandfather had an exciting business. He'd go to Africa, catch animals, and bring them back to distribute to all the zoos in North America. One summer, Linda went along with him delivering the zebras, giraffes, and other exotic animals all around the country. She remembers a time when she was sick and her grandfather would bring her animals for comfort. One time, he bought three little brown bears. Another time, he brought home a fawn, and still another time, a boa constrictor.

When her grandfather passed away, she became an animal trainer, landing her first job at Marine World Africa USA in San Francisco. She trained large cats—tigers and cougars—and worked with elephants, leopards, and bears. She later worked at the Seat Aquarium in Miami with killer whales and ended up as an elephant trainer at the San Diego Zoo. However, the pay was bad. "You're not making much more than ten bucks an hour, and you're laying your life on the line, especially with elephants," says Linda. She wanted to do something where she had equal job opportunity with men. She thought about becoming a zoo director or veterinarian, but felt these jobs would seem too much like desk jobs. So in 1978, Linda started flying, and eventually worked her way to an offer from American Airlines.

She was right about piloting being an equal-opportunity profession. "It's not a question of going out and having to network, it's strictly a matter of having a seniority number.

🌵 Cowgirl Spirit

You move up through the ranks based on that, and the type of airplane you choose to fly. Being a woman in flying is great today." In fact, some of the men she flies with now have wives and daughters who are up-and-coming pilots.

Linda feels as though the airspace is her land, and when she goes to her office—the cockpit—she has a fantastic view.

Airports have been lucky for Linda. While picking up her mother from a flight, she met the man her mother had been sitting next to on the plane. They ended up shaing a cab ride and a drink together. Later, he asked Linda and her mother out on a date. At thirty-seven, Linda married this man. Their son was born when she was forty three years old. Linda says, "Flying is hard on my home life because I leave a lot, but my husband is very understanding and wonderful and picks up the slack. My mother lives with us, which is rewarding in many ways, and she is home when I'm flying off some-where."

Linda is glad she had the experience of standing on the back of a dolphin, getting sat on by an elephant, and putting her head in the mouth of a killer whale. It all seemed phenomenal and amazing to her, especially since nothing was ever expected of her growing up. Linda found out for herself that "she sky's the limit."

Strength

Chapter Seven

Marriage

Life could be just a series of fates.
—Annabella Ransom, 1900

Then...

The marriage certificate reads, "What, therefore, God hath joined together, let no man put asunder." Over the man's photo on the certificate it proclaims, "It is not good that the man should be alone." (Gen. 2.18) Over the woman's, "I will make him an help meet [mate] for him." (Gen.2.18) It was traditional that a woman would marry, take care of her husband and bear his children.

Asa Mercer, self-proclaimed marriage broker of Seattle, was in Massachusetts speaking to a group of women and encouraging them to go west to seek their fortunes. He was aware of the scarcity of men and the need of these women to find themselves suitable husbands. Not only was Seattle in need of school teachers, tailors, and music teachers, but the city was swarming with young eligible men—men who not only felt the need for companionship, but were aware that the law entitled a man with a wife to twice the acreage to homestead. That, plus an extra set of helping hands, put the words "for better or worse" to continual testing.

Mercer offered accommodations to any woman willing to take the chance for one hundred fifty dollars and half price for children. They would travel by ship to the Isthmus of Panama, then take another ship to the Washington territory. He charged an extra fee to be paid by the husband once the marriage was consummated.

Ten ladies, ranging in age from fifteen to twenty-five, eagerly listened to Asa's talk and signed on for a chance at a better life in the west. This trip was most successful as all the women got jobs as teachers, with only one choosing to remain single as the others all quickly made their way to the altar.

On one of Mercer's trips, he had hoped to round up at least seven hundred passengers, but only came up with about one hundred, and of that group, only thirty-six were unmarried. The ship traveled clear around the tip of South America, and made its way north under grueling circumstances. The waters were choppy, the food scarce, and accommodations were of a very low standard. The ship passed through the Golden Gate and stopped in San Francisco. Unexpectedly, the port was filled with single men looking for wives, and married men sent by their wives to bring home cheap labor. Twenty of Mercer's girls took the opportunity and stayed in San Francisco.

There was much disappointment in Seattle, where rumors had been spread that hundreds of women were coming into port—so many that they'd have to ship some of them to Oregon. A mere handful of women got off the boat. One gentleman had requested Mercer bring a certain young girl from his home state. Unfortunately, the young woman who arrived wasn't the same girl, but just had the same name. No matter, the gentleman introduced himself and said, "I'm the feller that paid Mercer three hundred dollars for you to be my wife. I suppose you're as willing to get married this afternoon as any other time. I have to be home by sundown to milk the cows and feed the pigs." To his surprise, she replied, "You are impertinent! I paid my own fare, and I won't marry you." The suitor was puzzled. "If you didn't come to get married, what did you come for?" "I came to earn my own living as a tailor," she said, and turned and left him standing alone on the dock. Not for long, though, as another young woman saw her opportunity, and happily went off to her wedding. Another farmer looking over the women passed up the young, beautiful girls and picked a dour widow who had three strong-looking young sons. He proposed on the spot and they were married in three hours. In less than four, the boys were out working in the fields.

A most successful trip, thought Mercer, who married one of the passengers himself. These women from the east had been known in Seattle as Mercer Belles. When one, many years later, was asked to tell her story, she said, "Well, I never did anything special but give birth to eleven children, so I feel that I contributed to the population of Seattle."

Now...

Rachel Dunn was nineteen, but knew married life was for her. Eighteen years and three children later, Rachel still feels the same way. Rachel was a welfare baby. Her father died when she was ten years old, and her mother was left with five children to support. They were very poor, but her mother found joy in everything, played piano through all of the hard times, and made life fun for the family.

At fifteen, Rachel became a nanny for two children not much younger than herself. She loved them, and took the job to heart, but she had a goal. So, as soon as she turned eighteen, she packed up her truck with her brass bed and nightstand, and left for a singing career in Oregon. She worked in a restaurant, eventually auditioned for a band, and ended up marrying the drummer.

Mike came from a family with happily married parents, solid work ethics, and a beautiful home. He saw life differently than Rachel did. He was steady and secure. Rachel was always in survival mode, motivated by memories of not having money to feed herself or pay the rent.

The couple went into business together

selling firewood. Mike taught Rachel how to use a chain saw. They purchased Christmas trees from a farm in Oregon and drove them to Idaho every year. On the trips back, they would sell beans and potatoes to the Oregon market.

Even though Rachel often felt fearful, she was like her mother in many ways. She looked for the good and the fun in everything she did. If it was raining, she would enjoy the smell of the wet ground.

Always crazy about cooking, another skill she learned growing up, she decided to use this talent to start her own business. Her specialty was chocolate desserts. At age nineteen, she obtained a cottage industry license to make chocolates in her home. She started selling by knocking on doors of small businesses. The business began to grow, and Rachel was thrilled to be making money in her own kitchen.

Rachel recalls when she was pregnant with her son, John, and the smell of chocolate repulsed her. She could not hand-temper the chocolate herself, and Mike had to step in and do it all. The closest Rachel could get to that smell was delivering the finished and boxed product to customers. To this day, John does not like chocolate. "It's really a good thing that my husband and I are both involved in the business," Rachel says. "I love Mike and he adores me. I am so grateful every day for my life."

Her business was going well, but her sister thought she could do better in California. California sounded exciting to Rachel and Mike, so they decided to move. Rachel did extensive research to see if the business would be viable. She interviewed people in the coffee and gourmet

Cowgirl Spirit

foods industry, called editors of trade magazines, and shopped the stores. She was happy to find a market for her chocolates. Now, she needed to raise money for her venture.

She got help writing a business plan, sent chocolate invitations to customers and friends inviting them to come to an investors' meeting, and decorated the tables with piles of beautiful chocolates. Rachel presented her plan as she watched everyone happily eating the chocolates. She sold 40 percent of her company for a bankroll of $750,000. Grand Avenue Chocolates was ready to take the next step.

Together, Rachel and Mike bought equipment and set up a twenty-five-hundred-square-foot factory. Though Rachel was the candy expert, she knew nothing about equipment, and so Mike quit his general contracting job and became active in the business.

Although Rachel sells to large chains like Williams Sonoma, Saks Fifth Avenue, Bloomingdales, Neiman Marcus, and Nordstroms, they represent only 5 percent of her business. The mom and pop stores have always been her mainstay, and she is completely dedicated to them.

Media attention one holiday season sent Rachel's sales soaring. Oprah Winfrey recommended Rachel's three-pound Fuji apple—a dessert that serves about a dozen people, and is dipped in caramel, then dark chocolate and whole roasted almonds—a "must-have" for Christmas. The day before Thanksgiving, the apple was featured on *Good Morning America*.

49

Rachel does fifty-four gourmet trade shows a year. No matter how busy they are, for Mike and Rachel, the family takes precedence over everything else. At home there is no talk of work and no phone calls. The family sits together at the dinner table and talks for hours. It is the balance in Rachel's life.

Cowgirl Spirit

Chapter Eight

Children

If I have any more children, I'm goin' to be worn out. Ten is plenty for any woman.
—Dotty Mandy, 1875

Then...

Before 1849, there was no knowledge of ovulation, so there wasn't a way for women to avoid or predict pregnancies. Old wives' tales said that a woman could not conceive another child while she was nursing, but as many breastfeeding women found out, this was not to be relied upon. Not only were contraceptive methods difficult and unsure, but the whole issue was not talked about. Besides, women were often so isolated that it was impossible to pass information on to one another.

Delivery of babies happened in a variety of ways. One story tells of a teenage girl and her husband who delivered twins in a makeshift tent on the open plains during a blizzard. They had to wash the babies with ice melted in a pan. Miraculously, mother and babies survived.

Although many women married and had children in their early teens, some waited much longer to wed. Mary Richardson was one of these women, who, at twenty-six, was still unmarried. She wanted to have children and longed to be a missionary, but did not qualify because she was single. A sympathetic friend, however, knew of a shy farmer who also dreamed of a life in the missions, and who needed a wife. A

Cowgirl Spirit

meeting was arranged, and the next day Mary and the farmer married. His name was Elkanah Walker, and he was thirty-two years old.

The Walkers traveled by steamer and train to reach their destination. Hooking up with three other newlyweds, the couples traveled two thousand miles on horseback. Along the trail, Mary discovered that her husband had a bad temper—he was moody and melancholy. She wrote in her journal, "Should feel much better if Mr. W. would only treat me with some cordiality. It is so hard to please him I almost despair of ever being able to." Several days later she wrote, "Rode twenty-one miles without alighting. Had a long bawl. Husband spoke so cross I could scarcely bear it."

By the time Mary was pregnant, they were sharing a small house with several people, and privacy was nowhere to be found. She had her baby while Elkanah was on a trip. Many women did not have a physician at their delivery, but this time, Mary was lucky and one was available.

When the Walkers moved to a cabin of their own, Mary did all the cooking in the fireplace since there was no stove. She did little missionary work and preferred taking care of the baby.

On May 24, 1840, Mary woke up about four A.M. to help milk the cows. At eight o'clock, she gave birth to an eight-pound baby girl. The doctor couldn't get there and the closest midwife barely made it in time.

Mary worked hard. At nine months

pregnant with her third child, she awoke one morning at five A.M. to finish making the tallow candles she had started. Three day earlier, she had boiled mutton and beef fat and cooked it for several hours, then skimmed the impurities from the top of the pot and repeated the process. She had made a frame and hung twisted fiber from it. When this was finished she dipped the wicks into the melted tallow, cooled, and repeated the process until the desired thickness was reached. That morning, Mary made sixteen dozen tallow candles. Then she baked six loaves of bread, finished the housework, washed clothes, worked in the garden, and put suet up for pudding. That evening at nine o'clock, her third child was born. This time, the doctor arrived in time.

Now that Elkanah traveled, she began to miss him and he missed his family. He mostly missed the care she gave him and how she helped him when he got into one of those "blue moods." Missionary work became difficult because of hostilities of the Cayuses Indians, and the Walkers decided to leave for safer territory. They now had five children. Mary Walker bore her sixth child, a boy weighing nine pounds. The year was 1847. By 1852, Mary Walker had her eighth and last child. Altogether, she gave birth to seven sons and one daughter.

Although Elkanah had long suffered from stomach ulcers and "blue mood" attacks, the couple had become close and loving through the years. In 1877, Elkanah passed away. His last words were, "His loving kindness." Mary's diary read, "It seems as though I can't live without my husband. It is lonely to be a widow. I feel so lonely. Think so many things I want to tell Mr. Walker. I realize more and more how much more I loved him than anyone else."

When her children were grown and married, Mary began to teach Bible classes and attend lectures. She died at eighty-four years of age. She left five sons and a daughter, twenty-five grandchildren, and six great-grandchildren—all her pride and joy.

My ma always told me that anything is possible. —Jane Ralph, 1882

Now...

Toni Kirk feels that her biggest accomplishment in life is raising her children. She tells them never to give up their dreams, and that whatever they do is important. She surrounds them with a warm and loving home and teaches them to see beauty in themselves.

Toni's life didn't look that way when she was growing up. As the youngest of seven children, all one year apart, Toni's family was full of turmoil. Between relationship problems, money struggles, and alcohol abuse, she felt a lack of security from her parents.

Toni never remembers having her own room, nor even having her own bed. There were nights where she wasn't sure if she had a pillow or a blanket. She knew her mom was doing her best while trying to keep her own mental well-being intact. All of this made Toni mature very early.

Toni is a whirlwind mom with a typical day starting at 6:30 A.M. She'll meditate, fix breakfast for her two girls, and then drive them to school. She arrives at her part-time job at a clothing store by 9:00 A.M., and by 2:00 P.M. she's back at school to pick up her daughters, along with a few of their friends, and bring them back to her home for snacks, music, art, and homework.

Grocery shopping, washing clothes, cleaning house, and the other usual jobs moms do to keep the household together are just a part of her daily routine.

Toni, like many other modern moms, realizes that one of the essential requirements to being a good mother is to take care of herself. Toni found a great outlet to do just that when she joined a local soccer team. She never expected that she would end up helping her team become three-time champions. She explains, "Soccer makes me a better parent, a better wife, and I feel better about myself. It clears my mind and has taught me so much about teamwork. I was always told as a child that I was fragile, and so I was very intimidated by sports. I didn't want to believe that anymore, so I tried soccer. It's been a real joy and I've even been written up in the newspaper."

As a young girl, art and writing had a strong pull for Toni. Her dream this year is to take her art and writing into the world by illustrating and writing books for children. Because of her insecure childhood, she would like her books to teach children things that will help them early on so they don't accumulate negative feelings and emotions.

Toni always wanted to give her children things she never had; not material things, but the love and beauty she was seeking herself. Her husband, Jonas, provides their family with a sound life and the stability she never had growing up.

Toni knows that children learn by example, and she continues to work on herself so her girls will be strong, confident, and independent women. She encourages them to be open and communicate their feelings. Toni is getting tuned into what her life is about, and says, "Sometimes I feel that now I am living the childhood that I always wished I had."

My children have been a great comfort to me since their father is such a jerk.

Cowgirl Spirit

Chapter Nine

My Land, My Home, My Horse

The stars out here are so bright, I can ride
my horse anywhere at night.
—Edith Wright, 1862

Then...

Mary Ann Martin grew up working on her family's seventy-five-hundred-acre ranch in the Oklahoma Territory. She was a farm girl who learned how to ride when she was only four. Even as a child, Mary Ann loved to be outside with the horses. She could rope and shoot as well as any man—and better than some.

Like many ranch women, Mary Ann did a "man's work." She rode with cowboys in roundups and helped out on the family spread when men were in short supply. She would take to the saddle wearing buckskins and riding astride. This was scandalous, but no cowboy on the ranch would criticize her, as she was the boss' daughter.

Mary Ann preferred working the land to being in the home. She would break horses for other ranchers to earn a small sum. She was a good hand at branding, and even did some of the fence mending.

One afternoon, just after a heavy rain had ended, Mary Ann went out to the pastures to check on the cattle. As she approached the open land, she saw three men on horseback that she didn't recognize as ranch hands. Stopping, she watched them for a few minutes to find out why they were on the land. Then she realized they were cattle rustlers. Without hesitating, Mary Ann rode hard and fast to halt them. As she got close, one of the riders turned and saw that the rider chasing them was a woman. Before she could reach for her gun, he'd roped her off her horse. Undaunted, Mary Anne angrily whipped out her gun and pulled off a shot. She missed, but the gunshot drew the attention of the hired hands, who immediately came running. The rustlers fled at top speed. Mary Ann picked herself up, and, swinging her gun, said to the men, "The next time they come around, they won't be getting a second chance to do that to me." The men eyed each other, as if to say, "thank goodness it's not me she'll be after."

Mary Ann married at twenty. Her husband, George, was ten years her senior. They bought a large ranch, and Mary Ann continued to work the land until several years later when she gave birth to twins. She imparted her enormous mental and physical discipline to her boys by putting them on a horse as soon as they were old enough to climb onto a saddle.

Mary Ann remained a contented, healthy woman throughout her life, and at the age of seventy she could still be seen riding her horse confidently across the pastures.

My Land, My Home, My Horse

Now...

Anne-ly Crump-Garay was born in Sweden in 1945 to Estonian parents who had left Estonia during World War II searching for a better life. When Anne-ly was two years old, her family emigrated to Argentina, then left for Canada in 1951, where they settled and applied for citizenship.

By the time Anne-ly was six, she spoke four languages. Anne-ly felt the excitement of moving to all these countries even as a small child. She intuited from her parents that it was somewhat scary being displaced, but she still felt where her parents were was home to her.

When Anne-ly was in the fourth grade, she decided that she wanted to be a dentist. Her parents wanted a career for her that was going to be safe and steady, somewhat intellectual, but not too much so that she wouldn't be able to manage it. They wanted her to have what they saw as "feminine"—being a wife and mother—along with a career, which would give her an income. There were very few women dentists, however, in Canada in 1954.

Early on in her high school days, Anne-ly began to do public speaking. She remembers doing a speech on Rosa Parks for which she won a speaking contest, and began to feel that speaking publicly about people who were making a difference could make a difference in the lives of the listeners. Like many adolescent girls, life was hard for Anne-ly. She had periods of depression in her mid-to-late teens, a personal hardship she had to get through, which she considers her biggest challenge. She handled it by bearing through it and writing it out. When she looks back, this was probably her biggest challenge.

By the time Anne-ly met her husband, David, in a personal growth workshop in 1980, she had been married and divorced once, and was ready to begin a family if she could find the right mate. David was the seminar leader, and at the end of the workshop, Ann-ly invited him to go with her on a hot air balloon ride. Anne-ly says, "Ask 100 percent of the time for 100 percent of what you want and be willing to negotiate the difference. As long as we keep doing that, we will be a lot better off because people around us will be clear about what we want and need. There will be clarity and less resentment and unmet expectations."

David is seventeen years Anne-ly's senior. Their son, Christopher, was born when Anne-ly was thirty-nine. Moving around so much as a child, Anne-ly finally feels at home in a land she wasn't born in, and this is very important to her. On the other hand, she feels there is more that she can do for her adopted homeland, and she's not sure where that is going to take her.

Anne-ly is constantly looking to do things

My Land, My Home, My Horse

to give back to the land that has done so much for her. Christopher and Anne-ly have developed Project Read, a one-on-one literacy system for adults.

Anne-ly feels that for an immigrant child, she's done extremely well in the land she calls home. Anne-ly says, "I think I am incredibly fortunate and I am very grateful for my life and that I live in a wonderful place."

Chapter Ten

Hard Times

You'll learn nothin' if only
good things happen to you.
—Mary C. Clayaton, 1886

Then...

Cynthia Ann Parker was nine years old in May, 1836, when she was captured during a Comanche raid on her family fort. For years, relatives and friends searched for her, watching and listening to see if anyone saw a young white woman traveling with Indians. Once at a Comanche camp, a blue-eyed woman was spotted dressed as an Indian. The traders offered the tribe goods for Cynthia, but she ran from the men and hid. Cynthia was married now, and did not want to leave the tribe and her family.

Cynthia was twenty-four when she was next spotted. The English man who found her asked through an interpreter if she wanted to go back to her own people. Cynthia had lost her knowledge of English, had two Comanche babies, and was scared. She just stared at the man without replying.

In 1860, Texas Rangers attacked the Comanches. One ranger chased an Indian on horseback who was trying to escape with a young Indian girl clinging to his waist. The Ranger shot and hit the girl and the warrior, who both fell to the ground. He continued to fire at the warrior, mortally wounding him. The dead man was Peta Nocona, a Comanche war chief and the husband of Cynthia Ann Parker.

Cowgirl Spirit

Another Ranger captured Cynthia, who was tightly holding her baby daughter. Even though Cynthia had brown skin and dark hair, her eyes were blue, and the Rangers knew she was a white woman.

Cynthia was grief stricken about her husband's death and she did not know the whereabouts of her two sons. She clung to her infant daughter, who was still nursing. Cynthia felt that she had been captured once by Indians and now by the white man, and again taken from the people she loved. Even though she was reunited with members of the Parker family, she cried continuously.

Family members would ask her questions, but Cynthia would not answer. She did not care to learn English. She did, however, recognize the name Cynthia, even though her Indian name had been Prelock for years.

Cynthia did not feel like a white woman, and no one ever saw her smile again. She grieved for the loss of her husband and always dreamt of searching for her sons. Cynthia's grieving was intensified by the death of her daughter.

In 1864, Cynthia was sent to live with her sister in another country. She died from grippe at the age of thirty-seven, never knowing what became of her sons. One had died, but the other, Quanah, became a sub-chief of a Comanche tribe. Only fourteen when his father was killed and his mother captured, he was courageous and fought many battles, refusing to be ruled by the white government. One day, he came to the

Hard Times

—Sally Whitmore, 1889

I just can't work anymore today. It's been too rough.

conclusion that too many Indians were dying, and realized that, "If my mother could learn the ways of the Indians, I can learn the ways of the white man." He took his mother's last name, became a prosperous rancher, argued for the rights of the American Indian, and even rode in President Theodore Roosevelt's inaugural parade.

Quanah had his mother reburied on a reservation with his sister and later was buried beside her. Today, one can find monuments to Cynthia and her son on the old reservation.

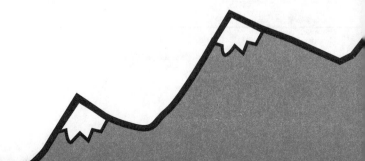

Now...

In spite of her difficult childhood, Carolyn Sirvinskas turned out to be a woman of consequence. The daughter of a "Southern Belle," she was told that there were things that were unacceptable for women to do. But Carolyn was a daring young girl. She played with the boys, climbing fences and flagpoles and jumping off the second story of her apartment building. She did all the things that boys did, and came to an early conclusion that men were allowed to do things that were much more fun than those allowed to women.

Carolyn came from an abusive family where her father beat her mother. He died when Carolyn was nine, and her mother remarried. Carolyn was thrilled to think that she finally had a family again, but this was short-lived when a male relative by this marriage began to abuse her. This continued until she was eleven years old.

The man threatened to harm her if she told anyone. She was very frightened and kept the secret to herself. She was determined to "act"

like a normal child so her mother would never suspect anything was going on. She developed herself much as an actress would prepare to play a part, measuring every small gesture or body language from others to determine whether or not they could see though her veil and discover her painful truth.

At eighteen, Carolyn went off to college. Her first year there, she met the man she was to eventually marry. He was a senior, and after his graduation, Carolyn left school with him. She worked many odd jobs before deciding to go back to college, this time earning her nursing degree. She found a job at one of the largest trauma center hospitals in Chicago.

At twenty-four, she still had never told the secret of her childhood abuse until her mother divorced her husband and Carolyn thought it was finally safe to reveal the molestation. Her mother was devastated, but ultimately, Carolyn's disclosure helped to open the door to a better relationship between mother and daughter.

Carolyn always drew great strength from her grandmother, Orlisie. Orlisie had lost a leg in a car accident at the age of thirty-eight. She was still a vibrant woman, and added one more child to her family after the loss. She taught Carolyn to remain open, to pay no attention to life's obstacles, and to keep going after what she wanted.

On a trip to Milwaukee, Carolyn and her husband walked into a small Native American store. At first, Carolyn wasn't particularly interested in the shop's contents, but she was mesmerized by the music playing in the background. She seemed to go into a trance, hearing voices chanting a language she didn't understand. Finally, her husband tapped her on the shoulder and broke the spell.

When she came out of this trance, she wanted to own everything in that shop. Everything that didn't attract her before became beautiful and desirable. This started her on the path to collecting Native American art and cowboy memorabilia. At the time, Carolyn didn't think about the fact that her grandmother had Cree Indian blood.

Carolyn decided that it was time for her to change her life's path. She felt she was coming out of the dark and becoming stronger and more sure of herself. She had finally left her troubled past behind and discovered her inner self. Now was her time to act without fear. She would leave nursing to start a new career.

Hungry to learn all she could about her new passion, she read everything she could find about Native Americans and cowboys. She read cowboy trading books that explained what a saddle was made of and she read about the history of spurs and boots. Books introduced her to frontier life and times. She picked up every western magazine she could find, sought out western movies, and was attracted to anything southwestern. When she took a trip to Santa Fe, New Mexico, she plowed through every shop.

Carolyn's determination to open up her own retail store almost broke up her fifteen-year marriage when her husband couldn't understand her desire to gamble their savings on her idea. Carolyn took a stand, and opened her store, Buffalo Gal Home Gallery, using money from her retirement fund. She started with a ten–by–ten–foot space at fairs and outdoor shows, and moved into a fifteen hundred–foot store location in Frankfort, Illinois. Her store is a huge success for her, and an affirmation that she got past the "hard times" in her life.

Chapter Eleven

Spunk

A cowgirl gets up in the morning, decides
what she wants to do, and does it.
—Marie Lords, 1861

Then...

Elsa Jane Forest Guerin was the illegitimate offspring of a bachelor Louisiana planter and his overseer's wife. Elsa grew up masquerading as her father's niece until he felt she was old enough to send her off to boarding school. It is no surprise, then, that Elsa Jane Guerin would grow up to be imaginative and resourceful.

At twelve, Elsa Jane married. She bore two children and was a happy housewife for four years. One afternoon, Elsa received a message that her husband was killed in a fight with one of his crew, a man named Jamieson. The man was brought to trial, but was not convicted.

At sixteen years old, Elsa Jane Guerin was left destitute and alone. She had no trade, and knew that work for women in 1846 was severely limited. Elsa decided to disguise herself as a man to seek employment. Sorrowfully placing her children into the care of the Sisters of Charity, she donned a male disguise and struck out to get work. Elsa also thought her disguise could serve a dual purpose to find her husband's killer and take revenge.

Elsa practiced speaking in a hoarse voice and started using rough language. "I buried my sex in my heart," she wrote. She was offered a job as a cabin boy on a steamer for $35 a month and accepted.

Once every month, Elsa would change into women's clothes and visit her children. Several times she thought of resuming her female role, but had financial concerns about her children's education. Besides, "I began to rather like the freedom of my new character. I could go where I chose, do many things which, while innocent in themselves, were debarred by propriety from association with the female sex. The change from the cumbersome attire of woman to the more convenient habits of man, was in itself almost sufficient to compensate for its unwomanly character."

Elsa became captive of her masquerade. Even when she was at home in St. Louis, wearing women's clothes and visiting with her children, she had trouble shaking off her acquired masculine ways. Sometimes at night she would don her male attire and wander around hotel lobbies, saloons, and steamboat decks. She could not resist even though her conscience argued against these trips.

On one of these evenings, Elsa spotted her husband's killer. She had purchased a revolver for just such occasion. She always said, "I would shoot him down as I would a mad dog." She followed him until they came to a quiet part of town, then challenged him. Elsa drew her gun and fired off a shot, winging her offender. At the same time, his shot wounded Elsa in the thigh. The man ran off, and Elsa hid in some nearby shrubbery, discovered as curious town folk ran to see what the commotion was about. The next morning, Elsa was given refuge by a widow who was sympathetic to her story. Elsa stayed with the widow until she recovered.

Spunk

I never lied to anyone I didn't have to.

In 1855, Elsa, still in disguise, joined a sixty-man expedition to California to look for gold. She didn't find strength to do this work in the winter rains, so she looked for more suitable work in Sacramento. A cleaning job in a saloon brought a $100-a-month salary. Elsa lived frugally, saved money, and eventually bought a partnership in the saloon. She sold out in eight months and began trading in pack mules.

Mule packing was a very profitable venture and Elsa sailed home for a short visit with her children. Later, she returned to California by organizing a train of fifteen men, twenty mules, horses, and cattle. The trip was difficult and there were many casualties. Elsa took her remaining funds and purchased a small cattle ranch in California, which she eventually sold along with her mule-freight business, cashing out at about $30,000. She told herself, "If I met with ordinary success I could retire into more private life, resume my proper dress, and thereafter in company with my children enjoy life to the full extent that circumstances would permit."

After a stay in St. Louis, Elsa realized that this idea no longer appealed to her, "I grew tired of the inactivity of my life and was determined to seek adventure in some new direction."

Again in men's disguise, Elsa worked for the American Fur Company, bringing pelts from the Indians on the North and South Platte rivers. She then opened an establishment in Denver called The Mountain Boy's Saloon and was known by her customers as "Mountain Charley."

Outside Denver one afternoon, as Elsa was riding her mule

Cowgirl Spirit

alone through a gorge, she saw a rider approaching her. At the same moment, the two riders recognized each other. It was Jamieson, her husband's killer. Elsa drew one of her six-shooters and knocked the man off his saddle with her first shot. "I emptied my revolver upon him as he lay, and should have done the same with its mate had not two hunters at that moment come upon the ground and prevented any further consummation of my designs." Elsa was so unnerved, that she failed to kill Jamieson. The man recovered only to die of yellow fever shortly after.

Before he died, he exposed Elsa to the Denver public. She immediately became famous and was relieved that her life as a man for thirteen years had ended. However, after all the years dressing as a man, Elsa still felt most comfortable in this attire. She continued wearing her male clothing until she eventually married the bartender who ran her Denver saloon and, who, until her exposure, had only known her as Mountain Charley.

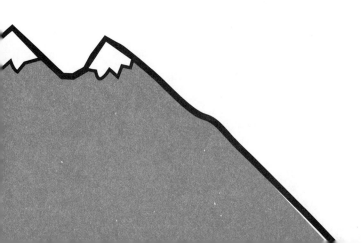

Now...

Karen Quest is a fire-eater, a juggler, a roper, and cracks a mean whip. But, what would you expect from a woman who graduated from the Ringling Bros. and Barnum and Bailey Clown College and won the Wild West Arts Club "Whipcracker of the Year" award in 1996? Karen always liked getting attention, and was a very outspoken, spunky young girl. Karen was a smart kid, but the cooperation column of her report card was always marked "Unsatisfactory," and her progress reports read "Talks too much."

Karen babysat every weekend of her life from the age of eleven until she was seventeen. She loved sitting in other peoples homes, reading Shakespeare and listening to folk music. Karen's family told her when she went to college that she was going to be a teacher and there were no other possibilities. So, Karen became an English major.

The school had a series of credit-exempt classes called The Experimental College. Karen took a class in clownology, and bravely went on a job to perform as a clown, where she met a woman who was a mime. She taught Karen how to juggle and together they performed street shows. Neither of them really knew what they were doing, but they had so much fun that they stayed at the park to watch other street performers.

Karen met a group of fourteen people called the Follies Mime Troop and invited them to stay in her two-bedroom apartment. She was intrigued with this kind of entertainment, and learned everything they were willing to teach her. Looking for more of this unique talent, Karen met some Navy boys who were unicycling in the park, and persuaded them to teach her how to ride a unicycle.

Karen's first professional juggling job was at Magic Mountain. Upon hearing that there was a magician eating fire in one of the theaters, she went to him to learn that skill.

Later, Karen decided that she wanted to join a company called National Theater of the Deaf, and tracked down a famous teacher of sign language at a local college. She switched her major to deaf theater because she just thought it was so exciting—a more pure, more direct, and more honest way of communicating. She realized because of her mime background that deaf people use mime constantly.

Karen dropped out of school and got a job at a restaurant where everybody had to be a performer. She had to audition just to be a busboy. Karen worked there for a long time performing comedy sketches, juggling, playing guitar, singing, and waiting tables.

After returning to school to finish her degree—she graduated with honors—Karen moved to New York and joined a clown theater company called the No Elephant Circus. Karen was very happy there, but the company folded. Karen went back to waiting tables and performing whenever she could. She joined the Juggling Association and learned everything she could

Spunk

about the craft. There, Karen met a woman who did performance tours with the Department of Defense. She had booked a tour and needed somebody to do it with her, as her two male partners were leaving. Karen accepted the challenge, and they left for Europe.

Karen loves the energy of performing in front of a live audience. "The audience is the ticket," she says. "It's that energy exchange." If somebody's life is enhanced for even one moment by her performance, she is satisfied.

Karen taught students at a circus school from ages four years old to ninety-three, and for the last decade, she has been teaching and performing. Karen's "Cowgirl Tricks" stage show is a western vaudeville act. She travels around the country performing her rope tricks and displaying her cowgirl humor. She rustles up a man on stage for the roping part of her act, and sends him hopping back to his seat completely tied up, with bull horns, a tail, and a cow bell around his neck. Karen can be seen standing on top of galloping horses or on stilts as an eight-foot cowgirl.

One of her biggest thrills is entertaining children who might be seeing a live perform-ance for the very first time. Karen will try something new at a drop of her cowgirl hat. She never listened to other people who told her that she shouldn't or couldn't do something and always follows her heart. One of Karen's favorite things about teaching is taking people from, "I can't do it," to, "I did it," exactly as she has done in her own life.

Cowgirl Spirit

Chapter Twelve

Aging

When I was a girl, I had dreams of becoming a woman.
Now that I'm a woman, I have dreams of becoming a girl.
—Agnes Mobley, 1898

Then...

Women on the plains lived and gave birth under harsh conditions—drought, dust storms, grueling labor, and fear of death or starvation. Isolation, depression, and plain hard work shortened the lives of many women, but others toughed it out and lived to a ripe old age, even thriving in those rough-and-tumble times.

Ranchwoman Tootie Brocker said, "I don't care if you're a hundred. Maybe your face looks like you're a hundred, but if you're bubbly, the age isn't going to show. Old ranchwomen have wrinkles from the weather, but that's not what you see. It's not what you look at."

Rodeo women, too, could still be going strong in their later years. Ruth Parton Webster entered her first relay race at sixteen. Ruth began to win the ladies' races, defeating some of the most talented riders. In 1917, she became one of the few women ever to win Frontier Days, the coveted *Denver Post* trophy for best female rider, in two consecutive years.

Ruth was hailed as the World's Champion Woman Relay Racer. The rough sport of relay racing required riders to race at full speed, stop instantly, switch their saddle to a waiting horse, jump on the horse's back, and race to the next relay station. This demanding routine is repeated until they reach the finish line.

Ruth Parton Webster retired from racing in 1929. At seventy-three, she still was training her own racehorses. She drilled, ponyed, and cared for them just as she did when she began racing thoroughbreds at the age of thirteen.

As sisters, Elsie Lloyd, born in 1897, and Amy Chubb, born in 1900, were slim look-alikes. They did all the work on their twenty-four-hundred-acre ranch that they bought with their husbands in 1954. Even after their husbands had passed away, Elsie and Amy continued to run eighty head of sheep themselves. They took care of as much as twenty-five hundred head.

Born in England, these sisters learned to ride at four years old. The family moved to Wyoming when the girls were fourteen and seventeen. They rode bareback and learned to jump. They both loved horses, and their early adult years were spent working roundups and breaking horses. They later became guides for deer and antelope hunters. The hunters stayed in housekeeping cabins on their land where the women say, "They damn well better cook for themselves."

After all, the sisters learned to do everything themselves. "You know, everybody says we've led such an interesting life. But it wasn't unusual to us. We just did it. That's what we had to do, so that's what we did," says Elsie.

Aging

Now...

Marjorie B. Conley, CEO of Nameplates Inc., is still making sales calls at the age of seventy-nine. "The word 'can't' isn't in my dictionary" she said.

Born in Tulsa, Oklahoma, in 1920, Marjorie was raised under the stern eye of her father, who was a farmer and a dairyman who became Country Commissioner for the city of Tulsa. "My two sisters and I had a very strict upbringing. Father was the ruler and we did what he told us too, but we adored him anyway."

In 1941, Marjorie married Robert Conley. Robert went off to the Air Force, and when he returned from World War II in 1945, he started his own printing company right from the kitchen in their home. They had three children, Robert Jr., Candace, and Claudia. Unfortunately, Robert Sr.'s health was not good, and he passed away in 1966. The youngest of the Conley clan was only nine at the time.

As most women who were raised in the twenties, Marjorie never expected to work, but the day after the funeral, she had to take over the family business.

Because of Robert's long illness, the company was not doing well and the debts amounted to two million dollars. But Marjorie was undaunted. She knew nothing about

🌵 Cowgirl Spirit

business, but she did know about honesty. "My father always taught me not to buy anything if I couldn't pay for it," she says. Marjorie is a highly intelligent woman, strong-willed and not afraid to work hard. She called all the company's suppliers and told them that if she didn't do what she thought she could do to pay off the debts, they could come and close her down. They believed she could keep her word. She made many personal sacrifices to keep the business operating. "You learn to ride with the punches, Honey," Marjorie said. In three and a half years, she was debt free, sold the business, and retired. Marjorie grew up with determination and discipline, and it paid off.

Marjorie enjoyed being home once more, but not for very long. One of the hardest times in her life was making the transition from being married and home with her family to becoming a working mother, but Marjorie liked the taste of business and received great satisfaction from the challenge. In 1973, just a year after she sold her business, she opened Nameplates Inc., a high-quality printing company specializing in metal etchings, flexible decals, and other grand-scale specialty printing. In 1986, Marjorie experienced one of the happiest moments in her life when she received two honors at once. She was named Tulsa's Small Business Person of the Year, and Oklahoma's Small Business Person of the Year. All state winners were invited to a reception at the Rose Garden at the White House. "This was probably the biggest honor of my life," Marjorie says.

"I think women should be prepared for something in their life, something where they use their own strengths. Women think they will get married and their husband will take care of them, but it doesn't work that way anymore. As you get older, you realize that we must be dependent on ourselves, not our family or welfare. Women should learn to do everything in the household, including balancing the checkbook." She advises any woman who decides to go into business to have enough capital to last three years, as it always takes more than you think to run your business.

Marjorie still works eight hours a day, five days a week, because she feels she can still do the job well. "It's common horse sense," she says, "that if you work long and hard enough, you can make anything work." Marjorie has made her company very successful and plans on working for the rest of her life.

Chapter Thirteen

Wisdom

If you have an imagination,
you can soar like a bird.
—Amy Anderson, 1897

Then...

The capture by Indians of white women was quite common. Some were never heard of again, but a woman named Fanny Kelly was wise about maintaining her survival and her hopes of rescue.

In 1864, while traveling to the Idaho Territory with her husband, Fanny was captured by Oglala Sioux Indians. Fanny was nineteen. She lived in terror and despair, afraid that her husband and niece were dead.

Immediately after her capture, Fanny became the property of Chief Ottawa, leader of the Oglala. He brought her to his tepee with his six other wives. The wives fought for the clothes that the Chief brought home from the raid, until they noticed Fanny's bruises and wounds. They stopped fighting and dressed her wounds.

The chief took Fanny to feasts and celebrations, and showed her off as his captive. She ate raw meat and dog stew. She was given many tasks and was made to celebrate the Indians' successes by dancing and yelling, holding poles with white men's scalps hanging from them.

Fanny prepared red willow bark for pipes, tended the wounded, learned the language, and translated stories from books taken from wagon trains. She was a wise girl and did whatever she could to make herself useful and convince the Indians that she was indispensable. Fanny feared for her life and it was threatened more than once. Chief Ottawa always defended her and said she was innocent.

The children loved Fanny, as she would sing for them and always smiled. Driven by jealousy, the chief's wives would make her life difficult. Fanny was constantly hungry, and did not find the meat of starved horses and dogs acceptable.

Fanny was asked by Chief Ottawa to write a letter to the leader of a military escort telling him that the Indians wanted peace. The chief's plan was to lure the men out of their fort, then attack them. Fanny didn't show her excitement, but she knew this was the time to warn the Captain of the plot and to beg for her rescue. She wrote the letter in English, translating the Sioux language so as not to use more words than the chief had spoken.

Over time, the Captain and his men offered money and goods for Fanny to no avail. They were determined to fight for her release. Later, when a delegation of Blackfeet Sioux wanted to sign a peace treaty, they were told that Fanny's release was a condition of the treaty.

The Blackfoot convinced the Oglala chief to let them use Fanny as a decoy. They brought Fanny 150 miles to their own village, and in December 1864, many months after Fanny's capture, a thousand

Wisdom

warriors headed towards the fort with Fanny to sign the treaty.

She was finally released and spent two months in the hospital recovering from frost-bite. Shortly after, her husband, Josiah, who had tried every way he could think of to free her, arrived at the fort. Fanny was shocked and overcome with emotion that her husband was still alive.

She received a five thousand dollar reward for warning the officers at Fort Scully about the attack plans of the Sioux. In the summer of 1865, Fanny and Josiah moved to Kansas and operated a hotel until he died of cholera in 1867. Fanny was pregnant, and soon after, gave birth to a son. She later sold the hotel and moved to Wyoming to live with friends.

While living at the home of her friend, Sarah Larimer, Fanny wrote a manuscript for a book. Later she came across a book with the title *The Capture and Escape: or Life Among the Sioux*. The author was Sarah L. Larimer. Sarah told everyone she would write about Fanny Kelly's capture in her second book. Fanny let it be known that it was her manuscript that was published, and, after taking legal action so Larimer's second book would not be written, Fanny finally had her book published. It was called *Fanny Kelly's Own Narrative of My Captivity Among the Sioux Indians*.

In 1880, Fanny remarried. She died in 1904 at the age of fifty-nine.

Now...

Cathy Bonner lives in Austin, Texas, and is a graduate of the University of Texas at Austin. She always did exactly what she wanted and knew how to accomplish whatever she started. Cathy was considered wise at an early age because of the way she approached getting things done.

Born in 1950, Cathy came from a very ordinary background. She was a middle child from a middle-income family. She and all her siblings started working at an early age. She always took it for granted that you work hard and try to accomplish what you can. Cathy is not afraid to take risks. She has been an entrepreneur all her life. She started and sold four different companies, including a cable company, a commercial construction company, a marketing firm, and a direct mail firm. Her father was a business owner and an entrepreneur, and Cathy thinks she inherited much of his strong work ethic. Her mother worked outside the home, so she figures that's where she got her independence. An idea of Cathy's was the Woman's History Museum in Dallas, Texas. The only comprehensive Women's History Museum to exist in the United States, it is affiliated with the Smithsonian Institution. Cathy sees this musem as a monument to women's wisdom, passed down through the ages. The museum project has raised twenty-eight million dollars, primarily through corporate and foundation grants.

Professionally, Cathy is a marketing consultant. For the last twenty-five years, Cathy has been a member of the Foundation of Women's Resources, an organization dedicated to bringing women's ways, perspectives, and wisdom to the workplace. Cathy helped start two programs, Leadership Texas and Leadership America. Subsequently, many other states have formed the same programs. Many women who have joined the leadership network on a national basis are now highly placed corporate executives.

Cathy's wisdom is evident to the people who work with her as she accomplishes the most difficult tasks with ease. "Nobody can do a large project alone," says Cathy. The phrase that Cathy lives by is, "No guts, no glory." She says, "Women shouldn't be afraid to try something new. Even if they fail, they are going to learn from it."

Chapter Fourteen

My Cowgirl Story

Place a picture of your own here.

_____

_____

_____

_____

_____

_____

_____

_____

_____

_____

_____

Cowgirl Spirit

Cowgirl Spirit

Published Sources

Bethenia Owens Adair: Some of Her Life Experiences, Mann & Beach, 1906.

Roger Conant. "Mercer's Belles," *The Washington Historical Quarterly.* University of Washington Press, 1960.

Dorothy Johnson. *Some Went West*, Dodd, Mead & Co. 1965.

The Library of Congress. *Pioneer Among the Spokanes*, The Caxton Printers, 1940.

Narrative of My Captivity Among the Sioux Indians, Donnelley, Gassette & Lloyd, 1880.

About the Author

Mimi Kirk was born and raised in Hollywood, California. She is the mother of four children and certainly has the Cowgirl Spirit herself. She was married at seventeen and widowed at twenty-nine; her youngest child was under a year old at the time.

Kirk became a student of Vedanta and then a devotee of Swami Muktananda. While she does not follow a particular tradition today, her spiritual life is central to everything she does.

Throughout her life, Kirk's talents and interpersonal skills brought her into numerous jobs and careers. She had a stint as a Las Vegas showgirl, and was the stand-in for Mary Tyler Moore in the 1970s hit sitcom *The Mary Tyler Moore Show*. She designed clothes and jewelry, and invented the popular scarf motif for Valerie Harper on the *Rhoda* series. After that, Kirk opened her own national jewelry manufacturing business, then became the regional marketing director for a company that delivered self-improvement seminars. She later became executive assistant and charity events coordinator for a private family, sat on the board of several nonprofit organizations, and was the founder, editor, and publisher of an environmental newspaper, *The City Planet*, in Los Angeles.

Mimi Kirk is the inventor of four board games, *Cowgirls Ride the Trail of Truth*, a board game for women eighteen to 118; *Cowgirls*, for teenage girls ages twelve to seventeen; *The Relationship Game: Love Starts Here*, which includes *The Little Book of Love*, for couples and singles; and *Big Happy Vacation: A Game of Family Discovery*. Kirk is currently the president of Side Saddle, L.L.C., the top relationship game company in the United States. Her games help support people in creating open communication, intimacy, self-knowledge, and kindness. You can find out more about these games by calling (888) 726-9447.